Published in English in Canada and the USA in 2021 by
Groundwood Books
First published in French in 2019 as *Tous les enfants ont droit à la
culture* by Rue du Monde
Copyright © 2019 by Rue du Monde
English translation copyright © 2021 by Groundwood Books

Groundwood Books / House of Anansi Press
groundwoodbooks.com

Groundwood Books respectfully acknowledges that the land on
which we operate is the Traditional Territory of many Nations,
including the Anishinabeg, the Wendat and the Haudenosaunee. It
is also the Treaty Lands of the Mississaugas of the Credit.

We gratefully acknowledge the Government of Canada for its
financial support of our publishing program.

With the participation of the Government of Canada
Avec la participation du gouvernement du Canada | Canadä

Library and Archives Canada Cataloguing in Publication
Title: I have the right to culture / words by Alain Serres ; pictures by
Aurélia Fronty ; translated by Shelley Tanaka.
Other titles: Tous les enfants ont droit à la culture. English
Names: Serres, Alain, author. | Fronty, Aurélia, illustrator. | Tanaka,
Shelley, translator.
Description: Translation of: Tous les enfants ont droit à la culture.
Identifiers: Canadiana (print) 20200392883 | Canadiana (ebook)
20200392891 | ISBN 9781773064901 (hardcover) | ISBN
9781773064918 (EPUB) | ISBN 9781773064925 (Kindle)
Subjects: LCSH: Children's rights—Juvenile literature. | LCSH:
Culture—Juvenile literature.
Classification: LCC HQ789 .S47513 2021 | DDC j323.3/52—dc23

The illustrations were rendered in gouache.
Printed and bound in South Korea

I Have the Right to Culture

Words by
Alain Serres

Translated by
Shelley Tanaka

Pictures by
Aurélia Fronty

GROUNDWOOD BOOKS
HOUSE OF ANANSI PRESS
TORONTO / BERKELEY

I am born on a day
that is sunny,
or rainy.

In this country,
or another one.

And the first thing I see
is eyes and smiles.

6

I hear gentle words
spoken in the language
of my family ...

I see shapes —
three, twenty,
a thousand ...

I recognize them —
tree, dog,
house, kiss ...

7

I like the smells that rise up
from cooking pots, from flowers.

I learn to name things
and then to count them.
I repeat the songs
my grandparents sing.

But soon I wonder about the children
who live somewhere else,
about the words they speak.
What games do they play?
What makes them laugh —
those children out there
in their homes so far away?

9

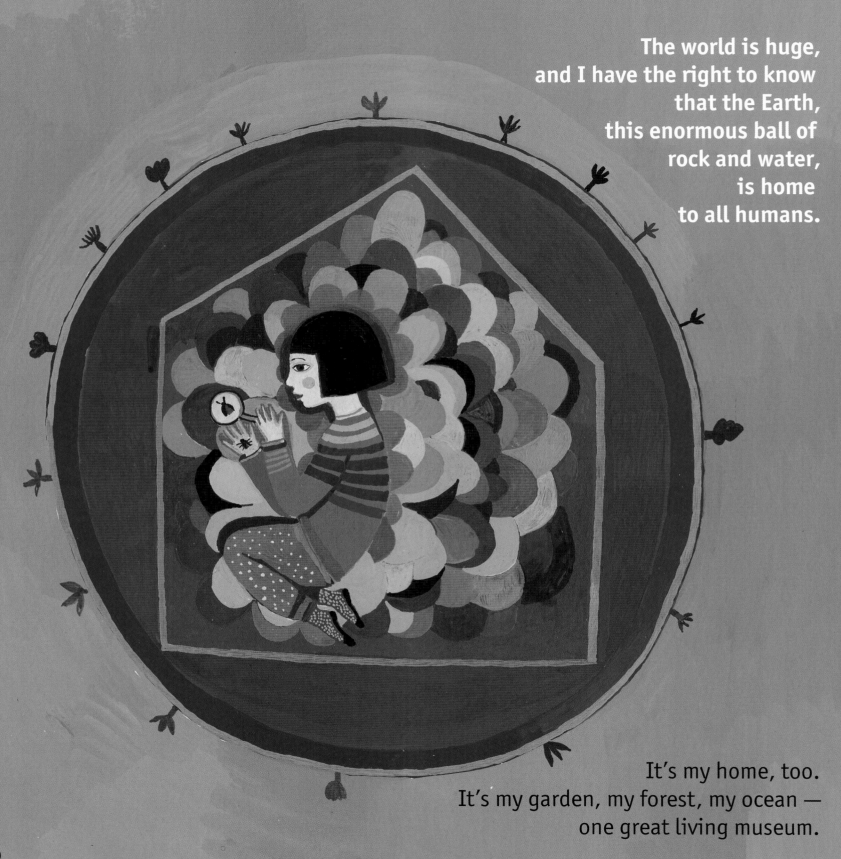

The world is huge,
and I have the right to know
that the Earth,
this enormous ball of
rock and water,
is home
to all humans.

It's my home, too.
It's my garden, my forest, my ocean —
one great living museum.

10

I have the right to know
the secrets
that hide in the heart of each flower
and in the shadow of each elephant,
so I can better protect every plant
and every animal.

Even the very smallest.

11

I also have the right to know everything
about the history of the world.

How did humans
learn to make
tools, clothes
and huts?

Why did they build
the pyramids,
put up statues?

How did they manage to make
ships that sailed on the sea?
To draw maps of the world?

How did they dare
to travel to unknown lands
by following the stars?

Why did they build castles for kings
who they would then overthrow?

Why didn't they forget
to invent jewelry?

A child who didn't know about
any of these things
would be a sadder child.

They would look at their hands
without understanding
where they came from.

14

I also have the right to know
everything about those billions of stars
scattered above the Earth.

The right to know
how we invented the telescope
that allows us to observe them.
And to know just how many
stars there are.

Look!
Here's an artist who paints
strange things
on his canvas.

Are those flowers,
or stars?
I ask.

And he answers,
I just paint.
You're the one who
decides what it means!

17

There are thousands of museums
around the world holding
works by hundreds of thousands of artists.

And can you buy them
the way you would buy flowers
from the florist?

Oh, no!
If you did that, other visitors
would no longer be able to
enjoy them.

**We can only take home
the way we feel about them.**

When we visit museums,
sometimes we want to paint, too.
To cut out and paste things ...

... because we all have the right
to create beautiful pictures,
even if we are not great artists.

There are also sculptors who make birds out of metal.

Video artists who film snails on umbrellas.

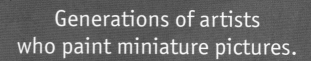

Generations of artists who paint miniature pictures.

And those who invent new street art.

The child who never knew about any of this,
who never walked around a sculpture,
never made black brush strokes on soft paper ...
would be as sad as a thousand birds who
never learned how to fly.

I have the right to
chat with one bird
by playing my flute,

to learn how to play the violin
so I can make friends
with two invisible crickets,

to make a special drum
that will amaze
three trucks,

or play the piano
with four hands.

... or imagine an orchestra
of seven billion musicians!

Oh, yes!

All the people in the world
would make music together.

It would be the end
of all wars.
Bravo for artists!

I have the right to love to dance,
even if I am rambunctious
or awkward.

Even if you dance like a human frog?
Ribbit, ribbit! Sure!
We're having a field party!

I also have the right
to watch a dance performance
for the first time in my life.

And for the second time in my life.

And maybe the hundredth ...

Ah, the acrobats, the clowns, the tightrope walkers!
Circus artists show us that if you work,
and work,
and work some more,
you can become as light
as the lightest feather ...

One day, will a juggler
be able to make our houses
float through the air
like a bouncy balloon?

Poets and writers
invent the world
they want to see.

They juggle the letters
of the alphabet and then ...

... they save their words
between
the pages
of a book.

33

Their books can then find their way
into bookstores and libraries
all around the world.

You can even meet authors who lived many years ago,
because the stories they invented live on in their books.

Sometimes those words start to speak!
They take on the voice
of actors
in plays
or in movies.

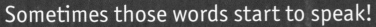

And what about me?
Do I have the right
to dress up
and go on stage, too?

Absolutely!
And your whole class
will applaud.

The child who could not experience
any of this would have every right
to be angry.

Art and culture,
all these treasures of humanity,
should be shared.

Too many children
do not get the chance.

When their family has no money,
when their school is too far away
for their small feet to walk,
they grow poorly,
like plants without fresh water.

37

Oh! I have an idea!
Maybe artists
could perform
a neat magic trick!

Three taps of a conductor's
baton, the stroke of a paintbrush
and a pencil crayon ... and, presto!
Everything would change.

38

Can you imagine?
Suddenly every child in the world could have
dance shoes,
a box of paints,
a ticket to attend the most wonderful puppet show ...

But since magicians
don't know this trick,
people will have to
do it instead.

Because the right to art, to leisure and to culture is written down
in the Convention on the Rights of the Child.
If we respect each word of this convention,
then every child will truly be respected, too.

The convention says that

CHILDREN — ALL CHILDREN — HAVE THE RIGHT TO DRINK CLEAN WATER ...
AND TO LISTEN TO THE FLOWING SOUNDS
OF BEAUTIFUL MUSIC.

THEY HAVE THE RIGHT TO EAT NUTRITIOUS FOOD ...
AND TO DEVOUR DELICIOUS BOOKS AS WELL.

THEY HAVE THE RIGHT TO BE CARED FOR WHEN THEY ARE SICK ...
AND TO DANCE IN CELEBRATION WHEN THEY GET BETTER.

THEY MUST NOT SUFFER FROM ANY KIND OF VIOLENCE ...
BUT THEY CAN FEEL ALL THE SWEETNESS OF POETRY.

CHILDREN HAVE THE RIGHT TO GO TO SCHOOL
TO DISCOVER BILLIONS UPON BILLIONS OF WONDERS
AND, IN THE COMPANY OF ARTISTS,
LEARN TO FIND BEAUTY IN THE WORLD.

Because to find
beauty in the world
is why children
are born in the first place,

on a day
that is sunny
or rainy ...

in this country,
or another one.

THE UNITED NATIONS CONVENTION ON THE RIGHTS OF THE CHILD

In 1989 the leaders of countries belonging to the United Nations General Assembly adopted the Convention on the Rights of the Child, a special code of human rights for children under the age of eighteen. It recognizes that children require special protection since they are more vulnerable than adults. Children have rights as human beings. They are not the possessions of their parents, nor should they have to depend on charity for their needs.

All of the rights in the Convention are based on the following criteria: non-discrimination (the rights apply to all children), what is best for the child, the right to live and grow in good health, and the right for children to express their opinions in matters that concern them.

The Convention is made up of fifty-four articles, each describing a right that governments have a duty to honor and fulfill, as should everyone else. Very broadly they include the right to water, food, shelter, education and healthcare; the right to be protected from harm; the right to take an active part in family, community and cultural life; and the right to grow to one's fullest ability. All of these rights are equal — one is not more important than another. The Convention also establishes benchmarks for healthcare and schooling as well as legal and social aid. In 2000, two Optional Protocols were added — one designed to protect children from taking part in armed conflict, and the other to protect them from pornography, prostitution and the sale of children.

So far 193 states — including every member of the United Nations except Somalia, the United States and the new country of South Sudan — are party to the Convention, having agreed to change or make laws and to develop practices and programs to support it. (Somalia and the United States have signed to show their support for the Convention but have not yet ratified it. The United States has ratified the two Optional Protocols.) Each state that is party to the Convention must report regularly to the UN Committee on the Rights of the Child, which monitors whether or not the states are complying. UNICEF and other non-governmental organizations work in many countries to help achieve the Convention's goals.

Since the Convention came into being, there has been more awareness of children's rights the world over. But there is still a huge amount of work to do. Children continue to be threatened by war, poverty, disease, drought and discrimination because of their religion, ethnicity, or because they are girls. And even in wealthy countries like Canada and the United States there are still many children without the basic food, shelter and clean water that they need. Many lack sufficient education and healthcare, and live with abuse and neglect. Children's rights are of the greatest importance. We all have a duty to insist that they be observed.

To view the UN Convention on the Rights of the Child go to
https://www.ohchr.org/EN/ProfessionalInterest/Pages/CRC.aspx

ALSO IN THE SERIES:

I Have the Right to Be a Child

An IRA Notable Book for a Global Society
A Children's Literature Assembly Notable Children's Book
A USBBY Outstanding International Book

In the first book in the series, a young narrator describes what it means to be a child with rights — from the right to food, water and shelter, to the right to go to school, to be free from violence, to breathe clean air, and more. The book emphasizes that these rights belong to every child on the planet, whether they are "black or white, small or big, rich or poor, born here or somewhere else."

Hardcover with jacket • ISBN 978-1-55498-149-6
EPUB • ISBN 978-1-55498-208-0

★ "Provocative and guaranteed to spark awareness of children's rights." — *Kirkus*, starred review

"[A] powerful work, and a handsome one." — *Publishers Weekly*

I Have the Right to Save My Planet

From the author and illustrator duo who created the award-winning *I Have the Right to Be a Child* and *I Have the Right to Culture* comes this beautifully illustrated picture book about a child's right to advocate for the environment they live in, as proclaimed in the Convention on the Rights of the Child.

Hardcover with jacket • ISBN 978-1-77306-487-1
EPUB • ISBN 978-1-77306-488-8

"A strong statement." — *Kirkus Reviews*